for family and friends...

39 things
to make a
cancer patient
smile

# Susan Reif

Inspired by the amazing and wonderful people in my life

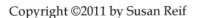

ISBN-13: 978-1461132080
ISBN-10: 1461132088

Design by Rosemarie Monaco of Group M Inc www.groupm.org

Printed by McNaughton & Gunn, Saline, Michigan, and CreateSpace

Discounts available on this book when ordered in quantity for bulk distribution or special sales. For more information, contact Susan Reif at Aunt's Enterprises at sbreif@gmail.com

*Hope is the thing with feathers that perches in the soul, and sings the tune without the words, and never stops at all.*

Emily Dickinson

# Acknowledgements

My hope is that everyone who is facing cancer has the love, friendship and network of caring people that I was so incredibly blessed to have. Thank you all from the bottom of my heart.

Mom, the best strength, support, care-giver, mom, friend and cheerleader anyone could ever have. You are the awesome one! Dad, I miss you every single day. Your overall strength and support, concern, and extra tenacity through the long trips in and out of the city, especially for the extra scary tests, helped get me through it all. G, my sincerest apologies again for the way the news was delivered, and my most heartfelt thanks for believing and schlepping out to Brooklyn with me! (it was the spark that re-ignited the fire for the book). Mom, Dad, and Gina, January 21, 2007 – the best family dinner… EVER!!! To Munch and Little Miss, the lights of my life -- thanks for the magic head rubs. To the Lewskis, the contest is over. We're all winners! Ellen, my dear friend who taught me so much about how to make a cancer patient smile. Ileen, whose choice in music kept me going. To Anne, who was at the door in a heartbeat. Claurice, a friend in need is a friend indeed. To the Moon Man, always. Joan, for all you did throughout, and also all the driving …from Chicago to Jersey and then Manhattan. Georgia, thanks for the travels! Roe, for believing in this book enough to design and help market it. Rhona, my mentor and friend. Carol, who drove and sat with me when I needed a ride. To my NAPL and AGAT Families, your hugs and multitude of smiles rocked. To Tammy, for your continual encouragement. Chris, the spa is calling! Joe, for having my best interests in mind. Robin, your light and kindness are greatly missed. Dr. Weiss, for the referral to Dr. Roses. To Dr. Roses for your expediency and urgency in getting me to Dr. Volm. To Dr. Volm for the seven words that changed everything: "You have every reason to be hopeful." To Nurse Peggy Kasper, a true angel. To Chemo Nurses Robin and Amy, and Social Worker Lisa, the work you do is truly inspiring. To Dr. Mitnick and Larissa, I wouldn't go anywhere else, twice a year. To the multitudes more, who were there in big and small ways, and continue to be there, sharing, caring and giving.

# Prologue

It started in late August 2006 with a routine mammogram. I was back in the New York area visiting family after a recent job relocation to the Midwest when I got a call-back after what was supposed to be a routine test. A full day of mammograms, a biopsy, a trip to the emergency room for uncontrolled bleeding from the biopsy, and soon it was September 12, 2006 for a follow-up visit to the doctor.

"It's Cancer," is all I remember hearing before I saw stars and had to be helped to the exam table. We had been waiting for 6 long days over the Labor Day weekend to find out the biopsy results, and when they came, they were earth-shattering. The second wait, and probably the more excruciating, was for the results of the full body PET Scan. That would determine whether the cancer was contained or had spread throughout the body. The good news, received via phone while in Wisconsin with my Mom, trying to pack up some things that I would need for the next few months while staying with my parents in NY: **it hadn't spread.** The initial prognosis was that the tumor was small and early. Subsequent tests however revealed that the cancer was Stage 3, large and extremely aggressive (though contained, thankfully) and would need to be treated quickly, extensively, and thoroughly.

My Dad described the whole process best. He likened it to a nice sunny day when you're walking down the street enjoying life, and out of nowhere, you get hit by lightning and are sent careening to the ground. That's the type of unexpected shock it was to receive all this news.

The next 2-1/2 weeks were a non-stop marathon of drives in and out of Manhattan (on an ideal day the trip was an hour each way… let's say the average was more like 1-1/2 each way.. to our record of 3 hours on a rainy Friday night…) for consultations, scans, tests, exams, blood work, PIC line insertion for the expedient delivery of chemotherapy, meetings with doctors, specialists, nurses, social workers, and hospital workers. The rest of the time was spent with family and friends, explaining, questioning, and gathering strength for the long journey ahead.

continued...

... Sixteen days after receiving the lightning bolt news, I was hooked up for my first of eight chemotherapy treatments. A treatment every other week. Just when you recover from one treatment, it's time for your next, and the cycle continues. To say the side effects are cumulative is an understatement, but progress was seen every two weeks, which kept me going strong.

More tests followed, one of which showed the cancer to have gone from 7mm to the size of a pinhead. So after a few weeks rest, the next step was surgery. After recovering from successful surgery, next came 42 radiation treatments. Soon it was May 1st and I danced around the maypole because the tests, scans, exams and blood work showed all was well! The tests and scans and blood work and exams continue on a regular basis with the oncologist, the surgeon, the radiologist, the gynecologist and the internist, and yes, thankfully, all continues to be well!

It was a long, hard nine months, but the support of family, friends, co-workers, acquaintances, business associates and strangers, made the journey a bit easier every day. I learned a tremendous amount about myself and those around me, and I learned that through all the challenges, people found ways to make me smile, every single day.

*Following are 39 of those ways that made me smile. I'm hoping you can use some of them to make others smile.*

# 39 things to make a cancer patient smile

Susan Reif

# Smile #1: Send Cards

Stock up on cards; funny cards, caring cards, blank cards, musical cards… you pick it. Start sending them as soon as you find out the person is ill. Keep sending them. Every week. Say things like, "thinking about you!," "sending a hug your way," "sending healing thoughts," "smile enclosed…" you get the idea. Just letting the person know that they're in your thoughts and prayers makes a world of difference.

There wasn't a day that went by over the course of my treatment that I didn't receive at least one card.

# 39 things to make a cancer patient smile

Susan Reif

# Smile #2:
# Tell Them Repeatedly How Awesome They Are

Cancer treatment is hard. Cancer treatment is challenging. Cancer treatment is not fun. Cancer treatment brings with it many physical and mental obstacles. Fighting cancer takes strength, determination, positive thinking and support (on top of all the medication!).

Everyone fighting cancer is Incredible. Amazing. Strong. Awesome. Remind them of that fact every day. My Mom told me every day how awesome I was, and she told that to everyone who asked how I was doing. She still maintains how awesome I am.

# 39 things to make a cancer patient smile

Susan Reif

# Smile #3:
# Send Customized M&M®s

What better way to make someone smile than chocolate with a personalized message. The ones I received from my sister said, "You did it!" "It's Gone." It was an incredible gift that lasted and lasted and made me smile!

She and I recently sent some to a friend and we learned an important lesson. The allowable messages can only be worded positively. When I politely told the woman on the other end of the phone that there was nothing positive about cancer, she told me I'd have to find a suitable message or she couldn't take the order… we ended up with "Beat Cancer." (What we really wanted to say was R-Rated and did not pass the M&M censors! You can use your imagination on that one…)

# 39 things to make a cancer patient smile

Susan Reif

# Smile #4:
# Make Something

If you're crafty or talented in the arts, now is the time to put that to use. From cards to needlepoint to knitting or anything in-between, a homemade sentiment is long remembered. I received many such things, including a beautiful butterfly made of crafts, pictures from kids, a quilt, a pillow made by the local elementary school children, and a box filled with hundreds of happy, positive thoughts and words on colored and decorated construction paper, along with confetti made of stars and other shapes. I still keep all these wonderful things around my home, bringing unending smiles!

# 39 things to make a cancer patient smile

Susan Reif

# Smile #5: Offer to Drive

They may have a network of drivers lined up to take them to appointments, tests, treatments, updates, etc., and they may never take you up on the offer, but they will long remember that you did offer. Don't assume that they are set for a ride. We met a woman in the doctor's office who had just received the news that she was sick. She was instructed to set up a variety of appointments in the coming weeks, several of which she would be unable to drive to and from because of the extent of the procedure. She lived alone in the city, and spent nearly 30 minutes trying to arrange for a ride. She was in tears, overwhelmed and unable to confirm a ride. My Mom and I were rendered to tears watching this woman struggle to find assistance from family and friends.

Here's the lesson: if the patient does need a ride, and you can provide it, you will have done a wonderful thing which will never, ever be forgotten. Ever.

# 39 things to make a cancer patient smile

Susan Reif

# Smile #6:
# Gift Cards Go Far

Not sure what to send or bring. Gift cards are a special treat. It doesn't have to be a lot and it doesn't have to be from anyplace fancy. It's a gesture that they're thought of. When they're feeling well, it's fun to go and spend it. If not, they can use it online and receive packages! Pick a store you know they like, or pick a fun new website. I received a lot of bookstore gift cards (my guilty pleasure) and had a wonderful time spending them.

# 39 things to make a cancer patient smile

Susan Reif

# Smile #7: Books

There are lots of books about cancer, and chances are, if the patient is interested in reading them, he or she will have already done so. My recommendation, pick out books that help the patient escape: a mystery series; a crossword puzzle book; a book of jokes or laughter; biographies; classics. Check to make sure that the book doesn't feature a cancer patient. You don't have to go out and buy new books. Look at your bookshelf and pull a favorite out to loan. Go to a used book sale and buy a few. Be creative!

# 39 things to make a cancer patient smile

Susan Reif

# Smile #8:
# Make a Music Mix

Cancer treatment is tiring. Patients often rest for long periods of time. It's nice to have some music to listen to… a special mix for a special person. During my treatment, a dear friend loaned me her iPod. It was like I had landed in the musical archives! There was every type of music imaginable on there. Anything I could think of was there, and the selection kept me busy and happy for many months! You may not want to loan away your iPod, but you certainly can make a mix of music for the patient, especially if music has played a part in your relationship.

# 39 things to make a cancer patient smile

Susan Reif

# Smile #9: Bring Food

This one's a bit trickier, so it's best to ask first.
There were many things I couldn't eat during
treatment, but there were still many choices.
Ask first also because chemo wreaks havoc on
the patient's taste buds…. But having said that,
it was nice when someone called up and asked
if they could bring lunch over. I had some
funny cravings during chemo, and if anyone
asked what I wanted for dessert, the answer
was always the same: Yodels®, please! Comfort
food; maybe. Find out what they're craving,
and deliver it! Or, make your specialty comfort
food and bring it in a freezer-proof container.
The patient will have a future meal which he/
she will be very grateful for.

# 39 things to make a cancer patient smile

Susan Reif

# Smile #10: Flowers: Live and Virtual

Flowers brighten anyone's day. Send a "thinking of you" bouquet. Nothing beats live flowers, but if that's not in your budget, there are plenty of websites now that send free virtual bouquets. You can decorate a card online to accompany the virtual flowers and definitely make someone smile.

# 39 things to make a cancer patient smile

Susan Reif

# Smile #11: Call

Get over being uncomfortable. Pick up the phone and call. Say hello, I'm thinking about you. Don't not call because you are concerned that they may not want to talk. If they don't want to talk or they are not feeling well enough to talk, they won't answer the phone, or they'll tell you, or they'll have someone else tell you. Don't be discouraged; don't take it personally. Know that if you call, and even if they can't talk to you, you have helped make their day easier. Knowing that someone is thinking about them during their difficult journey is very comforting.

# 39 things to make a cancer patient smile

Susan Reif

# Smile #12:
# Help Out at Home

There were days when it took every ounce of energy I had to get out of bed and put on sweatpants and a sweatshirt. (Forget about the wig!) How nice it was not to have to worry about cooking a meal or cleaning up on those days.

# 39 things to make a cancer patient smile

Susan Reif

# Smile #13:
# Help Out at Work

When I got sick, my co-workers jumped in and were amazing. I did my best to stay involved, and was able to accomplish a tremendous amount working from home, but my friends and co-workers in the office went above and beyond to help out with projects and deadlines and ensured that things were successfully accomplished.

# 39 things to make a cancer patient smile

Susan Reif

# Smile #14:
# Get Yourself Checked

It's a fact. When someone is diagnosed with cancer, it spurs the people in their circle to get checked. As I mentioned, in my case, the cancer was discovered during a routine mammogram. It can happen to anyone. And it does. So if a friend or family member is diagnosed with cancer, learn more about detection and make sure you get checked... regularly.

# 39 things to make a cancer patient smile

Susan Reif

# Smile #15:
# It's OK to Be Afraid

Hey, cancer sucks and it's scary as hell.
And you wouldn't be human if you weren't
scared. But here's the thing... the patient is
facing the biggest challenge of his/her life
and now is the time for you to summon
your courage, gather your strength, and
show your support. It will be difficult, but
not nearly as difficult as what the patient is
going through.

# 39 things to make a cancer patient smile

Susan Reif

## Smile #16: Send Prayers, Angels

No matter what somebody's beliefs are, all the prayers and hopes of others are welcomed! I received angel figurines in all sizes and shapes and they are proudly displayed around my home, reminding me of the care and concern of others.

# 39 things to make a cancer patient smile

Susan Reif

# Smile #17: Visit

Call first. There are good days and bad days. If the person is not up to a visit, don't be offended. Try again. Once there, monitor the length of your visit based on the patient. They'll be happy to see you; but be sure to take your cues from them regarding the length of your stay.

# 39 things to make a cancer patient smile

Susan Reif

# Smile #18:
# Out for a Drive, Out for Lunch, Out...

On good days, what a treat it was to get out! If the patient is not up for lunch or shopping or an activity, a drive is always a good option. No particular destination required. The patient will be very happy to just be out and about.

# 39 things to make a cancer patient smile

Susan Reif

# Smile #19:
# Support the Cause

One month after I was diagnosed, my mom, sister and dear friend participated in a "Walk for the Cure." I can't begin to tell you how touched I was. I still get teary-eyed every time I think about it.

If you can't do something like that, a small donation in the person's honor goes a long way. Some of my favorites are NYU Langone Cancer Center, Stand Up To Cancer, and the American Cancer Society. There are many, many organizations in need of donations... all searching for treatments and cures. Do your research, then contribute your time or make a donation. You could even ask the patient where they'd like the donation made. Every dollar counts.

# 39 things to make a cancer patient smile

Susan Reif

# Smile #20:
# E-mail, E-cards, Text Messages, etc.

This by far is the easiest and fastest way to keep in touch. Send a quick message, again just letting them know that they are on your mind. Do it often. Spread a little kindness quickly!

# 39 things to make a cancer patient smile

Susan Reif

# Smile #21:
# Keep Them Up to Date with Your Life

The overriding subject on a patient's mind is his/her treatment schedule, tests, results, the disease, the progress... you get the idea. It will be a very welcome change for them to hear all about what's going on in your life. Really, it's important for them to get out of the moment for a while. Nothing is too trite; don't measure your words against the enormity of what the patient is going through. Your life and its activities are important and interesting. Don't stop sharing. The patient wants to know and stay involved.

# 39 things to make a cancer patient smile

Susan Reif

# Smile #22:
# Send Pictures

What better way to keep someone involved in your life than through pictures? There will be many events that the patient misses due to treatment or effects. By sending pictures, they can feel as though they were there. And it doesn't have to be a special event. Send everyday shots of your family or friends. All will be appreciated.

# 39 things to make a cancer patient smile

Susan Reif

# Smile #23:
# Figure Out What They Need Done and Offer to Do It

It may be something simple like picking up something for them at the grocery store or pharmacy. It may be helping them get organized with their paperwork. It may just be they would like some company. Ask them; they'll tell you what they want or need. Or, if you listen very carefully, you may find that an opportunity presents itself.

I was talking on the phone with a friend, and the topic of my car came up. I was explaining that we were in the process of figuring out how to get my car from Wisconsin back to New York. I had left it there at my apartment when I came back to NY for treatment. I told her that two members of my family were going to drive

continued...

# 39 things to make a cancer patient smile

Susan Reif

...out together, pick up the car, and drive back. As I was relaying the story, my friend, who lived in the NY Metro area said, hey, I am going to be in Chicago; can you get your car to Chicago and I'll drive it back to NY. Turned out another friend in Wisconsin was able to drive the car to Chicago (along with my some things I needed from the apartment), and the first friend drove it back to NY.

In my wildest dreams, I would never have asked someone to do that for me. In my mind, it was above and beyond and then some. What an amazing help it was and my family and I are still grateful that she offered her assistance.

# 39 things to make a cancer patient smile

Susan Reif

# Smile #24:
# A Vicarious Trip

I share this story with the permission of a wonderfully creative friend who provided me a journey around the world while I was going through treatment! Shortly after I was diagnosed, I started receiving postcards showing pictures of places near and far. Each contained a story featuring the imagined adventures we were having in that particular location. One postcard was from a spa, and it told of the pool, the massages, the facials and other relaxing treatments taking place! No matter what was going on for me, when those postcards arrived, I was transported away from cancer and from reality for a little while.

continued...

# 39 things to make a cancer patient smile

Susan Reif

...How did she do it? She had an associate whose business it was to print postcards, and he graciously shared the overages with her. While not everyone has access to these types of connections, there are similar things you can do. Go on the internet and print out some pictures of places and create your own stories. Or use magazine or newspaper clippings. Or even photos from past trips. Anything to give the patient a bit of an escape will be tremendously appreciated.

# 39 things to make a cancer patient smile

Susan Reif

# Smile #25:
# The Human Touch

Human touch is so crucially important to anyone's well being… especially someone fighting a terrible disease. Don't be afraid to reach out and touch their hand or shoulder or give them a hug if they are up to it. (If you're unsure, ask first.) But please, please, please, stay away if you are sick or have been exposed to anything contagious recently.

A cancer patient's immune system is being crushed to smithereens by the chemotherapy and because of that, he or she becomes very susceptible to becoming sick. It is crucial for the patient to stay as strong as possible or the chemo schedule may be put in jeopardy. You don't want to be the cause of that! Wash your hands frequently and thoroughly, and wear a mask or stay away until you are well.

# 39 things to make a cancer patient smile

Susan Reif

# Smile #26:
# The Magic Head Rub

This is not for everyone. And this certainly is only for those very close to the patient. Please don't attempt this unless you have a close relationship and you know that it would be welcomed.

My niece was not quite 3 and my nephew was 7 when I was diagnosed. They knew I was sick, and they knew that the medicine was making me tired and in pain, and had caused me to lose my hair. They wanted to do something to make me feel better when I was lying in bed, and they came up with the magic head rub. Imagine four small hands gently rubbing my bald head and telling me the magic would make me feel better. You know what, it sure did make me feel better, and it sure did make me smile.

# 39 things to make a cancer patient smile

Susan Reif

# Smile #27:
# Movies Pass the Time

Watching movies and going to the movies are
great escapes from the realities of the world.
Invite the patient to the movies (keep it light)
or if they're not feeling up to going out, rent
a few (or borrow them from the library) and
drop them off. You can stay and watch if
invited, or you can pick them up and return
them. Again, make sure that no characters
in the movie are dealing with cancer or long
illnesses or tragedy. Now is the time for
comedies and happy endings only.

# 39 things to make a cancer patient smile

# Smile #28:
# Become the Best
# Listener Ever

Sometimes, the patient will want to talk. If
and when they do, be the best, most active
listener ever. A dear friend taught me long
ago that if you listen long enough, you will
learn everything you need to know. If you're
looking for ways to help the patient, if you
are an engaged listener, you'll hear what you
can do for them. Sometimes, it's just an ear
that they need.

# 39 things to make a cancer patient smile

Susan Reif

# Smile #29:
# Offer to Accompany
# Them to the Doctor

Even if they are set for a ride to the
doctor, make sure they are not going to
appointments on their own. Even today, there
are still some appointments that I cannot go
to by myself. I like to think that being this
many years removed from the experience
allows me some perspective, but the fact is I
can't foresee the day when I'll be able to go
for a mammogram without the support of a
loved one. The trauma resurfaces, and having
someone there is a tremendous help.

# 39 things to make a cancer patient smile

Susan Reif

# Smile #30:
# Remember Important Dates

Important dates in the life of a cancer patient are very different than important dates for a well person. Life becomes driven by a new schedule, consisting of doctor's appointments, tests, exams, scans, etc. and the results associated with them. If the patient shares those dates with you, make a note to follow up with them afterward.

# 39 things to make a cancer patient smile

Susan Reif

# Smile #31: Fleece Caps

Many cancer patients lose their hair during chemotherapy, and while wigs are wonderful, there are days when you just don't have the energy to put them on. That's when very soft, very comfortable fleece caps come in handy. My favorites are the Land's End watch caps. They come in a variety of colors and they make great gifts. Pick a few colors, order online or via phone, include a nicely worded gift card, and the patient will receive them in a few days. I guarantee, the caps will quickly become a favorite with the patient, and they're especially great on cold winter nights.

39 things to make a cancer patient smile

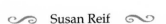

Susan Reif

# Smile #32:
# Be a Steadying Force Through the Roller Coaster of Emotions

As things progress with treatment, new options, scenarios, and scares are presented to the patient. With me, progress was immediate and continual, but there were some curve balls along the way.

One of those curve balls was the genetic testing. I had been rolling along, seeing positive improvements and focusing on that. Then, we had the genetic testing conversation. I immediately agreed to do it, wanting to provide information for my mother, sister and niece, hoping against hope that my cancer was not hereditary, thereby reducing challenging decisions for them. During one of my chemo sessions,

continued...

**67**

# 39 things to make a cancer patient smile

Susan Reif

...the geneticist explained the process, reviewed the potential outcomes and drew blood for the test. What I wasn't prepared for were the potential decisions I would be faced with based on the outcome of the test. While waiting for the results of the expedited test, my emotions took a nose dive. I shared that with very few people, but the few that I did again made all the difference. They listened, they supported and they reminded me that no matter what, I was not alone. As family and friends, sometimes during the journey you are called upon to be supermen and superwomen in supporting the patient. You can do it.

P.S. My results showed that my cancer was not hereditary, thereby eliminating the need for any major decisions, and eliminating the need for my Mom, sister and niece to go through the testing process.

# 39 things to make a cancer patient smile

Susan Reif

# Smile #33: Stay Strong & Do Things for You

Sounds like words for the patient, but caregivers, friends and loved ones need also stay strong. Take time for yourself. Continue your routines as much as possible. The stress of an illness is not limited to the patient, so be sure to be kind to yourself… as often as possible.

The patient will definitely feel better knowing that their illness isn't all-consuming, every day, to those around them. It will absolutely make the patient smile to know that their caregivers get a break to relax and enjoy.

# 39 things to make a cancer patient smile

Susan Reif

# Smile #34:
# Everyone is Different

I learned this lesson early on. My cancer, experience, treatment, and side effects were unique to me. There are many types of breast cancer and there are a variety of treatments, and while there are many similarities, everybody reacts and responds differently. The patient learns this as she/he goes along, talking to doctors, nurses, social workers, technicians, and hearing from others who have had cancer.

continued...

# 39 things to make a cancer patient smile

Susan Reif

...As the friend or family member, what you can do to help the patient is not over-share the cancer and treatment experiences of others you have known (unless they specifically ask). As helpful as you might think this may be, it can create the opposite response for the patient. When I was going through treatment, the only cancer-related stories I wanted to hear from outsiders were ones that had happy endings. But you'd be surprised at how often other tales arise. Think first of the patient and their need to stay positive before sharing.

# 39 things to make a cancer patient smile

Susan Reif

# Smile #35:
# Do Group Projects

Groups of friends pooled their ideas and
resources and sent sources of sunshine on
a regular basis. Big and small packages
arrived, filled with things like a fluffy
soft bathrobe, lotions and creams, scented
heating pads, edible fruit bouquets,
stuffed animals, and lots of other creative
and fun gifts. As each package arrived,
another smile was elicited!

# 39 things to make a cancer patient smile

Susan Reif

# Smile #36:
# Celebrate Little Victories Along the Way

Cancer treatment is a long journey. There are highs and lows. In order to keep going, all successes, all small improvements, all positive signs have to be acknowledged and celebrated along the way. Keep in touch with the patient and help celebrate these little victories. It may be an interim test result, or reduced negative side effects, or reduction in the size of the tumor, or simply that the patient had a really good day. Find a way to make a big deal about it.

# 39 things to make a cancer patient smile

Susan Reif

# Smile #37:
# Create Rituals

As I mentioned, cancer treatment tends to take over a person's life. It's nice to have some special time or special rituals that help take the patient's mind off the current reality. For me, there were several. My Dad was a night owl, and a TV junkie. During my treatments I had trouble sleeping, so there were many nights we watched *The Tonight Show* and *The Sopranos* together. Even after my treatments were over, and I moved back into my own house, I would return on Sunday nights to watch the *Sopranos* with Dad, and would check in with him in the morning regarding Jay Leno's previous night's guests.

Another ritual was playing Cribbage®, Scrabble® and Boggle® with my Mom. She's the Cribbage champ, but I still give her a run for her money on the word games!

# 39 things to make a cancer patient smile

Susan Reif

# Smile #38:
# Do What You Can
# But DO Something

Anything is better than nothing. Know This:
Any gesture of kindness, small or large, will
be immensely appreciated. We all have busy
lives, and we all get wrapped up in our day-
to-day activities of family, work, obligations,
etc., but now is the time to become one of
those people who goes out of their way to
remember others and extends a hand.
Do Anything. Do Something.

# 39 things to make a cancer patient smile

Susan Reif

# Smile #39:
# Just Be There

*Enough Said!*

# 39 things to make a cancer patient smile

Susan Reif